go, go, GRAPES!

A FRUIT CHANT

by april pulley sayre

Beach Lane Books
New York   London   Toronto   Sydney   New Delhi

For Carolyn, Reid, and all the Pulley bunch

Thank you to the South Bend Farmer's Market, where much of this fruit was photographed. Special thanks to the Hovenkamps, Marie, Kay, Klug's, Vaughn and Carol of Wolf Farms Perennials & More, Johnson's Produce, Disterheft, and Wolf Farms & Greenhouses. Local grocers Gini and Gene Bamber of Bamber's Superette, Alfredo Palacios of El Paraiso, Oanh and Bao Nguyen of Saigon Market, and the crew at Shelton's Farm Market sourced exotic fruit and allowed me to photograph displays. Blueberry Ranch, thanks! During my travels, other food folk welcomed me and helped too: Whole Foods in Chicago; Jungle Jim's International Market in Hamilton, Ohio; Daley Plaza Farmer's Market in Chicago; Crescent City Farmer's Market in New Orleans; the Vietnamese Farmer's Market in East New Orleans; Kitchener Market and St. Jacobs Farmer's Market in Ontario; Jean-Talon Market in Montreal; and the Ecology Center Farmer's Market in North Berkeley. Thank you, Mary and Gordon. Mango smoothies to Andrea, Isabel, Candace, and Jeff for their support, and to Lauren for the juicy, joyful design.

BEACH LANE BOOKS • An imprint of Simon & Schuster Children's Publishing Division • 1230 Avenue of the Americas, New York, New York 10020 • Copyright © 2012 by April Pulley Sayre • All rights reserved, including the right of reproduction in whole or in part in any form. • BEACH LANE BOOKS is a trademark of Simon & Schuster, Inc. • For information about special discounts for bulk purchases, please contact Simon & Schuster Special Sales at 1-866-506-1949 or business@simonandschuster.com. • The Simon & Schuster Speakers Bureau can bring authors to your live event. For more information or to book an event, contact the Simon & Schuster Speakers Bureau at 1-866-248-3049 or visit our website at www.simonspeakers.com. • Book design by Lauren Rille • The text for this book is set in Calvert. • Manufactured in China • 0312 SCP • First Edition • Library of Congress Cataloging-in-Publication Data • Sayre, April Pulley. • Go, go, grapes! / April Pulley Sayre.—1st ed. • p. cm. • ISBN 978-1-4424-3390-8 (hardcover) • ISBN 978-1-4424-3391-5 (eBook) • 1. Grapes—Juvenile literature. 2. Children's poetry. I. Title. • SB388.S29 2012 • 641.3'4—dc23 • 2011011602 • 10 9 8 7 6 5 4 3 2 1

Rah, rah, raspberries!
Go, go, grapes!

Savor the flavors.
Find fruity shapes!

**Blackberries. Blueberries.
Bag a bunch.**

Strawberry season?
Let's munch-a-munch!

This BOOTH Same Family AND FARM FOR Over 40 Years!

Michigan ORGANIC STRAWBERRIES $25 PER FIAT

Hello, tangelo!
Tamarillo shines.

Cactus and kiwano—
prickly spines!

Cheer for cherries,
tart or sweet.

Bananas. Oranges.
Peel and eat!

Ask for apples, round and ripe.

Try them. Pie them.
Red. Green. Stripe!

Pineapple. Pomegranate.
Take your pick.

Yell for yumminess:
kiwis—quick!

Grab a guava.
Live for lime.

Pucker up, pal,
it's lemon time!

Nectarines, tangerines,
hit the spot.

Glum? Go plum.
Or apricot!

Try a papaya.
Rambutan—romp!

Mango. Mangosteen.
Chomp, chomp, chomp!

Grapefruit. Dragon fruit.
What a find!

Cantaloupe. Watermelon.
Mind that rind!

Figs are fabulous.
Currants call.

Love a lychee—
fruit eyeball!

Reach for peach.
Fuzz is fine.

Pluck a persimmon.
Then, durian dine!

Share a pear,
picked by hand...

**treats from trees
and from the land.**

Baskets. Bushels. Seasons. Sun.
Feel it? Peel it!

Fruit

is fun!

Fruit for Thought

Plants produce fruit to attract animals. Fruit is filled with seeds. In nature, animals help spread seeds as they tear apart fruit, eat it, and carry it away. The colors, tastes, and smells that make fruit attractive to wild animals make many fruits tasty to people, too. Over thousands of years, farmers have bred fruit to make it easier to grow and to ship to fruit fans in different parts of the country—and the world.

Gulp That Pulp

Fruits are naturally full of vitamins, minerals, and fiber. Berries, especially, are health champions. Their deep colors indicate high concentrations of antioxidants, compounds thought to be helpful in fighting disease. Nutritionists recommend eating a balanced diet with plenty of fruits and vegetables.

Befriend a Fruit!

Shapes. Textures. Colors. Smells. Fruit is art you can eat! So why not become the "fruit artist" for your family? Read about a fruit. Learn to serve it. Offer to wash, peel, and set out fruit snacks. Decorate plates with colorful slices. Make a smiley face, a bicycle, or even spell out words! But beware: Fruit goes fast. You might want to capture your art with some "fruitography" before the munching begins....

Fruit That Didn't Make the Cut

Fans of cranberries, loquats, and other fruit not included in this book, please don't feel crushed. You can find these and other fruits, fruit facts, and fruit photos at AprilSayre.com.

No fruit was harmed or mistreated in the making of this book. Some did, however, end up in a jam.